*GREATER ....
ALSO AVAILABLE IN EBOOK AND
AUDIOBOOK FORMAT.

Greater Than a Tourist Book Series Reviews from Readers

I think the series is wonderful and beneficial for tourists to get information before visiting the city.

-Seckin Zumbul, Izmir Turkey

I am a world traveler who has read many trip guides but this one really made a difference for me. I would call it a heartfelt creation of a local guide expert instead of just a guide.

-Susy, Isla Holbox, Mexico

New to the area like me, this is a must have!

 -Joe, Bloomington, USA

This is a good series that gets down to it when looking for things to do at your destination without having to read a novel for just a few ideas.

-Rachel, Monterey, USA

Good information to have to plan my trip to this destination.

-Pennie Farrell, Mexico

Great ideas for a port day.

-Mary Martin USA

Aptly titled, you won't just be a tourist after reading this book. You'll be greater than a tourist!

-Alan Warner, Grand Rapids, USA

Even though I only have three days to spend in San Miguel in an upcoming visit, I will use the author's suggestions to guide some of my time there. An easy read - with chapters named to guide me in directions I want to go.

-Robert Catapano, USA

Great insights from a local perspective! Useful information and a very good value!

-Sarah, USA

This series provides an in-depth experience through the eyes of a local. Reading these series will help you to travel the city in with confidence and it'll make your journey a unique one.

-Andrew Teoh, Ipoh, Malaysia

>TOURIST

GREATER THAN A TOURIST-
MASSACHUSETTS
USA

50 Travel Tips from a Local

Kathryn Clark

Greater Than a Tourist-Massachusetts USA Copyright © 2021 by CZYK Publishing LLC. All Rights Reserved.

All rights reserved. No part of this book may be reproduced in any form or by any electronic or mechanical means including information storage and retrieval systems, without permission in writing from the author. The only exception is by a reviewer, who may quote short excerpts in a review.

The statements in this book are of the authors and may not be the views of CZYK Publishing or Greater Than a Tourist.
First Edition
Cover designed by: Ivana Stamenkovic
Cover Image:

Image 1: By King of Hearts - Own work, CC BY-SA 4.0, https://commons.wikimedia.org/w/index.php?curid=62981160
Image 2: By Terageorge - Own work, CC BY-SA 3.0, https://commons.wikimedia.org/w/index.php?curid=22552968
Image 3: By User:Expos1225 - Own work, Public Domain, https://commons.wikimedia.org/w/index.php?curid=1600384
Image 4: By en:User:Shinkuken - English Wikipedia, Public Domain, https://commons.wikimedia.org/w/index.php?curid=4768912

CZYK Publishing Since 2011.
CZYKPublishing.com
Greater Than a Tourist

Lock Haven, PA
All rights reserved.
ISBN: 9798722872272

\>TOURIST

\>TOURIST
50 TRAVEL TIPS FROM A LOCAL

BOOK DESCRIPTION

With travel tips and culture in our guidebooks written by a local, it is never too late to visit Massachusetts. Most travel books tell you how to travel like a tourist. Although there is nothing wrong with that, as part of the 'Greater Than a Tourist' series, this book will give you candid travel tips from someone who has lived at your next travel destination. This guide book will not tell you exact addresses or store hours but instead gives you knowledge that you may not find in other smaller print travel books. Experience cultural, culinary delights, and attractions with the guidance of a Local. Slow down and get to know the people with this invaluable guide. By the time you finish this book, you will be eager and prepared to discover new activities at your next travel destination.

Inside this travel guide book you will find:

Visitor information from a Local
Tour ideas and inspiration
Save time with valuable guidebook information

Greater Than a Tourist- A Travel Guidebook with 50 Travel Tips from a Local. Slow down, stay in one place, and get to know the people and culture. By the time you finish this book, you will be eager and prepared to travel to your next destination.

>TOURIST

OUR STORY

Traveling is a passion of the Greater than a Tourist book series creator. Lisa studied abroad in college, and for their honeymoon Lisa and her husband toured Europe. During her travels to Malta, an older man tried to give her some advice based on his own experience living on the island since he was a young boy. She was not sure if she should talk to the stranger but was interested in his advice. When traveling to some places she was wary to talk to locals because she was afraid that they weren't being genuine. Through her travels, Lisa learned how much locals had to share with tourists. Lisa created the Greater Than a Tourist book series to help connect people with locals. A topic that locals are very passionate about sharing.

TABLE OF CONTENTS

Book Description
Our Story
Table of Contents
Dedication
About the Author
How to Use This Book
From the Publisher
WELCOME TO > TOURIST
ANIMALS
1. NEW ENGLAND AQUARIUM
2. STONE ZOO
3. FRANKLIN PARK ZOO
4. THE BUTTERFLY PLACE
5. DAVIS FARMLAND
BREWERIES
6. NAVIGATION BREWERY
7. STONE COW
CAPE COD
8. THINGS TO DO AND PLACES TO GO ON THE CAPE AND ISLANDS
9. PROVINCETOWN
10. HYANNIS
HISTORICAL SITES
11. LOWELL NATIONAL HISTORICAL PARK

12. LEXINGTON AND CONCORD
13. FREEDOM TRAIL
14. OLD STURBRIDGE VILLAGE
15. ADAMS NATIONAL HISTORICAL PARK
16. SALEM
17. DEERFIELD
18. PLYMOUTH PLANTATION

MUSEUMS

19. MUSEUM OF FINE ARTS
20. ISABELLA STUART GARDNER MUSEUM
21. CHILDREN'S MUSEUM
22. WORCESTER ART MUSEUM
23. ECOTARIUM
24. NORMAN ROCKWELL MUSEUM
25. BERKSHIRE MUSEUM

SPORTS

26. FENWAY PARK
27. CELTICS
28. BRUINS
29. REVOLUTION
30. PATRIOTS
31. LOWELL SPINNERS
32. WOO SOX

AMUSEMENT

33. SIX FLAGS
34. APEX

>TOURIST

35. MGM
36. ENCORE
37. PLAINRIDGE

HIKES

38. QUINCY QUARRY
39. PURGATORY CHASM
40. GREAT BROOK FARM

TIPS, TRICKS AND MISCELLANY

41. PURPLE PLUME
42. HOW CAN I BE GOING SOUTH WHEN I AM HEADED NORTH?
43. SPEAKING OF HIGHWAYS
44. RECOMMENDED RESTAURANTS
45. PLACES TO STAY
46. LINGO
47. TOWNS AND CITIES
48. WINTERS
49. SUMMERS
50. ARRIVING IN THE STATE

Did you Know?

Other Resources:

Packing and Planning Tips

Travel Questions

Travel Bucket List

NOTES

>TOURIST

DEDICATION

This book is dedicated to my mother, Edna, who had the foresight and strength to emigrate from a tiny hamlet in New Brunswick Canada to the state of Massachusetts.

>TOURIST

ABOUT THE AUTHOR

Kathryn is a wife, mother and teacher who lives in Lowell, Massachusetts and loves to try new adventures.

Kathryn loves to travel…

Kathryn Clark is a lifelong resident of Massachusetts. That is except for the 2 and ½ years she lived in nearby Maine and New Hampshire in her early 20s. In her teen years she could be found at the local McDonald's where she worked or at the local mall. That is where she spent the money she earned working.

Kathryn is currently a Social Studies teacher in Lowell, Massachusetts. She has lived there since the early 1990s where she and her husband raised two boys. They recently kicked them out of the nest to go and start their own lives and are now empty nesting. This is of course after an addition was added to their home, because why not? In all fairness the project was started before the boys moved out. After the construction loan was secured and planning had begun, the youngest announced he had joined the Navy and left for boot camp. Soon after the foundation was poured the oldest announced he took a job in Florida and then he moved out. So Kathryn and her husband now have a large empty house for just the two of them. They lovingly await for grandchildren to fill the empty space, though they are not holding their breath for that to happen any time soon.

    Kathryn has a creative side and writing is one part of it. She also enjoys painting, crocheting and sewing. You can check out Kathryn's blog http://nearlyemptynesting.weebly.com/ to read sweet, sentimental and sometimes snarky observations of her life.

>TOURIST

HOW TO USE THIS BOOK

The *Greater Than a Tourist* book series was written by someone who has lived in an area for over three months. The goal of this book is to help travelers either dream or experience different locations by providing opinions from a local. The author has made suggestions based on their own experiences. Please check before traveling to the area in case the suggested places are unavailable.

Travel Advisories: As a first step in planning any trip abroad, check the Travel Advisories for your intended destination.
https://travel.state.gov/content/travel/en/traveladvisories/traveladvisories.html

FROM THE PUBLISHER

Traveling can be one of the most important parts of a person's life. The anticipation and memories that you have are some of the best. As a publisher of the Greater Than a Tourist, as well as the popular *50 Things to Know* book series, we strive to help you learn about new places, spark your imagination, and inspire you. Wherever you are and whatever you do I wish you safe, fun, and inspiring travel.

Lisa Rusczyk Ed. D.
CZYK Publishing

>TOURIST

```
WELCOME TO
> TOURIST
```

Boston

Worcester

>TOURIST

Springfield

Cambridge

11

>TOURIST

*"Talk about the life in
Massachusetts
Speak about the people I have
seen"*

~ From the song "Massachusetts" by the Bee Gees

Massachusetts, also known as the Bay State, is full of interesting places to visit and explore. It has great hikes, quaint little towns, bustling cities, historical and literary sites just to name a few. There are a variety of art and science museums throughout the state as well. Many communities, such as Lowell, have growing artisan populations. Lowell has many hip galleries and art studios to visit. WIth history, art, technology and nature Massachusetts has a lot to offer.

In 1620, the Pilgrims settled in Plymouth making them the first English settlement in what would become Massachusetts. Massachusetts Bay Colony was founded in 1629 in Boston. These two colonies combined by 1691 forming the Province of Massachusetts. The Patriots in Massachusetts played a pivotal role in gaining independence from England by organizing boycotts and protesting taxes. After the American Revolution, Massachusetts became the sixth state to join the United States on February 6, 1788.

During the nineteenth century, Concord, Massachusetts saw great literary minds of Emerson, Thoreau and Alcott and the birth of Transcendentalism emerged into the world. By the twentieth century, Massachusetts was a bustling center of technological companies, research facilities and institutes of higher learning. Here we are today in the early parts of the twenty-first century and looking forward to what great things we will see here in the state over the next eighty or so years.

Many colleges and universities call Massachusetts home including Harvard University, the oldest place of higher learning in the United States. Harvard was established in 1636. The University of Massachusetts system has many great schools throughout the state, including one Lowell.

The state of Massachusetts has a population of 6.8 million people as of 2019 and is roughly 10,565 miles squared. While it is the fourth largest of the New England States, Massachusetts ranks 45th in size for the entire United States. The geographic center of the state is in the town of Rutland in Worcester County. Massachusetts is bordered by New Hampshire and Vermont in the North, Upstate New York to the west, Connecticut, Rhode Island and part of the Atlantic Ocean on the south and the Atlantic Ocean to the East. The state of Maine was once part of the state of Massachusetts. It separated from Massachusetts when the Missouri Compromise added the state of

>TOURIST

Missouri as a slave state to the Union. Maine was added as a free state.

Some famous firsts that happened in Massachusetts. A few of the firsts include the first Thanksgiving in 1621, the first American Public Library in 1653, the first abolitionist newspaper - The Liberator in 1831 and the first computer developed in 1928 at Massachusetts Institute of Technology.

Massachusetts has a lot to offer for people looking for an exciting vacation.

Massachusetts is broken into the following regions:

Boston and MetroWest- This is Boston and the surrounding suburbs about twenty miles west of Boston.

North Shore- The area North of Boston, sometimes known as Cape Ann.

South Shore- The area South of Boston

Cape and Islands - This area includes Cape Cod, Martha's Vineyard and Nantucket

Central Mass- This area encompasees Worcester and the cities and suburbs to the north and south.

Connecticut Valley- Sometimes called Pioneer Valley, this part of the state is in between Central Mass and the Berkshires.

Berkshires- This is the western part of the state in the Berkshire Mountains. It borders upstate New York.

This book is divided into different topics of things to do and places to visit here in the Bay State. This is just a small part of what is available to do in the Great State of Massachusetts.

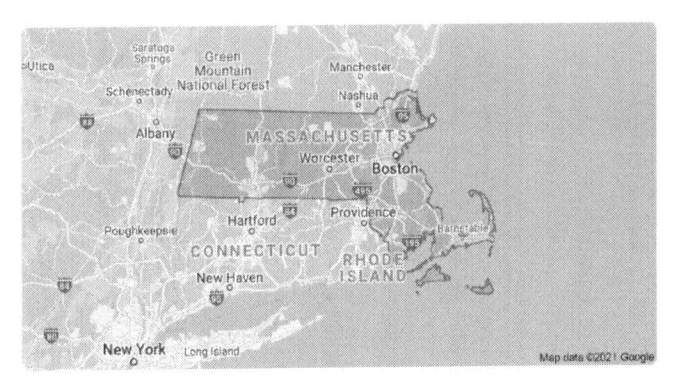

Massachusetts
United States

>TOURIST

Boston Massachusetts Climate

	High	Low
January	37	22
February	39	24
March	46	31
April	57	41
May	67	50
June	77	59
July	82	66
August	81	65
September	73	58
October	62	47
November	52	38
December	42	28

GreaterThanaTourist.com

Temperatures are in Fahrenheit degrees.
Source: NOAA

>TOURIST

ANIMALS

1. NEW ENGLAND AQUARIUM

The New England Aquarium is located in Boston at 1 Central Wharf. Current prices of admission are $30.00 for seniors, 60+, $32.00 for adults and $23.00 for children 3-11. Children under 3 and aquarium members are free.

The New England Aquarium has a great penguin exhibit. There are more than 70 penguins living in this exhibit and over 150,000 gallons of water from Boston Harbor. Of the 70 penguins there are two species, African Penguins and Southern Rockhoppers. When I was a kid there was an advertisement on television for the NE Aquarium. As I sit and type this, a part of the commercial is stuck in my head. All I hear over and over right now is,"I can walk like a penguin." a line that was on the commercial that played over and over in the 1970s.

The Giant Ocean Tank is the main exhibit at the New England Aquarium. A spiral walkway with viewing spaces encircles this tank taking you up four stories to the top. Inside the tank you will find sea turtles, all kinds of fish, eels and stingrays. The coral reef is home to hundreds of Caribbean sea creatures. Make sure you make it all the way to the top of the exhibit. It is quite a site to see.

Don't miss the Atlantic Harbor Seal exhibit as you walk into the aquarium and the seal show at the Marine Mammal Center. Also, make sure you don't miss the many smaller exhibits and hands on experiences as you stroll through the aquarium.

2. STONE ZOO

The Stone Zoo is located at 149 Pond Street Stoneham, MA. Summer hours are from April 1- September 30. The zoo is open between 9:00 am to 5:00 pm weekdays and until 6:00 pm on weekends. October 1- Mach 31 the zoo is open for their winter hours, 9:00 am to 4:00 pm.

Current admission rates are $16.95 for adults, $15.95 for seniors 62 and older, children ages 2-12 are $10.95. Children under 2 are free.

There are many different animal exhibits to see from barnyard animals including goats and chickens to Himalyan Highlands where you can see a snow leopard or a yak. And then everything in between.

I fondly remember taking my boys to the Stone Zoo when they were younger. My boys found it interesting that the coyote exhibit was adjacent to the road runner exhibit. The Looney Tunes reference did not get past them. Beep! Beep!

>TOURIST

3. FRANKLIN PARK ZOO

The Franklin Park Zoo is located at 1 Franklin Park Road Boston, MA. It is part of the New England Zoo system with the Stone Zoo. The hours are the same as Stone Zoo, however current admission rates are $18.95 for adults, $16.95 for seniors 62 and older and $12.95 for children 2-12 years of age.

In warmer weather make sure to visit the Giraffe Savannah to see, you guessed it, zebras! Ha Ha. Of course giraffes are there too. Make sure to visit the Serengeti Crossing where you will see ostriches and warthogs and head over to Outback Trail to see the kangaroo.

There are a few seasonal exhibits as well. The Aussie Aviary opens in the warmer months as does Butterfly Hollow.

4. THE BUTTERFLY PLACE

Speaking of Butterflies, you may enjoy a visit to the Butterfly Place located at 120 Tyngsboro Road Westford, MA. This is a seasonal business that is open from 10:00 am- 4:00pm from Mid February to Early October.

Current admission prices are $14.00 for adults, seniors 65 and older $12.00 and children between 3-

12 years of age are $10.00. Children 2 and younger are free.

As you walk around inside, remember a few things. It is kept at a temperature between 80-85 degrees in the butterfly flight area. As you walk through the flight area you will observe a variety of butterflies flying around you. There is no place to eat inside The Butterfly Place, but there is a nice picnic area outside. Don't forget to bring your camera for some fantastic photo ops.

5. DAVIS FARMLAND

I first heard of Davis Farmland when my boys went there on a field trip in preschool. It is a great place for families. Davis Farmland is located at 145 Redstone Hill Sterling, MA. It is a seasonal business that is open in the Spring through the end of October. Davis Farmland policy states that adults must be accompanied by a child 12 or younger. Davis Farmland is a place for children to learn about animals through experiences and play. Children can take a pony ride, learn about milking cows, taking care of chickens and other farm animals, take a hayride and pick apples and pumpkins in the fall . There is also a small water play area, a playground for climbing and bouncing and a place to order lunch

>TOURIST

Davis Farmland also has a phenomenally fun interactive corn maze each year in September and October. Each year the corn maze has had different themes such as the movies or pirates. The maze is multidimensional with bridges and activities built within the maze itself and covers acres of land. The activities connect directly to the yearly theme. When the boys were no longer interested in the farm side, they were still always excited about going to the Davis Corn Maze each fall. My oldest son was born in September. This was always a fun way to spend his birthday with a few of his friends. Corn mazes are not easy though. One may find themselves in there wandering around for up to 2 hours. Don't worry if you get hungry. A snack bar is built into the maze, there is always staff to offer help and lots of things to discover and do. This event has evolved over the years and is now called Davis Mega Farm Festival. This festival includes live music, craft beer and Kansas City BBQ.

>TOURIST

BREWERIES

6. NAVIGATION BREWERY

Navigation Brewery is located at 122 Western Ave Lowell, MA. It is in the Western Ave Studios. Navigation is open on Thursday- Saturday from 4:00-9:00 pm and on Sundays from 12:00-5:00 pm.

While they do not serve food at Navigation Brewery, you won't go hungry. There is always a food truck available outside. Navigation encourages you to bring your food into the establishment.

In the warmer months, the patio at Navigation Brewery is open to the public. Sit outdoors and enjoy a game of cornhole with your beer. The Brewery is pet friendly.

Navigation Brewery is located in Western Ave Studios. Do not miss the opportunity to explore the different art galleries before enjoying your cold beer. The first Saturday of every month is open studios from 12:00-5:00. Check out the amazing artists and enjoy the different genres and mediums that they work in.

7. STONE COW

Stone Cow Brewery is a recent discovery of mine. After a hike with some friends in Barre, MA we ended up at the Stone Cow Brewery for lunch. I was amazed at how beautiful the surroundings were.

Stone Cow Brewery is located at 500 West Street B, Barre, MA. You can't miss it. There literally is a stone cow out in front. Stone Cow Brewery is open on Friday and Saturday from 12:00-6:00 PM and on Sundays from 12:00-5:00 PM.

Stone Cow has a place to sit down and order food and of course beer. There is also a little shop to buy some merch. Outside at Stone Cow Brewery is a nice small area for kids to play.

Massachusetts has many breweries throughout the State. If you find one you like, let me know so I can go and check it out!

>TOURIST

CAPE COD

8. THINGS TO DO AND PLACES TO GO ON THE CAPE AND ISLANDS

If you go to the Cape and Islands there are plenty of places to visit if you need a break from the beach. Here are just a few of the many things you can do on Cape Cod.

Head to the Wellfleet Drive-in for a bit of nostalgia and a double feature every night during the summer. This is a great place for families. Make sure to arrive early to get a good spot.

Heritage Museum and Gardens located in Sandwich on the Cape has a little something for everyone. Tour the 100 plus acres of gardens, ride the vintage carousel, visit the kids section called Hidden Hollow for their own adventure. Explore the collection of folk art and collection of antique cars.

Also in Sandwich is the Sandwich Glass Museum. Here you will see both modern and historical displays of glass and witness glass blowing demonstrations. Hours of operation vary based on the season.

In the mood for some summer theater? Visit the Cape Playhouse in Dennis. This playhouse has a famous group of alumni actors including big names like

Gregory Peck and Humphrey Bogart. The production quality of the shows is top notch. The theater is in an old meetinghouse. Despite the rustic appearance it is a great place to catch a show.

Looking for a different kind of adventure? Head to Cape Cod Inflatable Park. Ok, this may be more of an adventure for you kids, but why can't you have some good old fashioned fun too? Cape Cod Inflatable Park is located in West Yarmouth. Hours vary based on the season. Climb, bounce and slide your way into a good time.

Visit one or all of the sixteen lighthouses on the Cape.

Take a scenic ride on route 6A and see the magnificent houses and sites on the Cape.

Head to Truro Vineyards for a tour and a wine tasting.

Hop on a ferry and explore Martha's Vineyard. Once you are there head to the Aquinnah Cliffs, Edgartown Lighthouse and stop by and see the bridge from the movie Jaws.

Take another ferry to Nantucket. Check out the Nantucket Shipwreck and Lifesaving Museum, The Whaling Museum or wander among the stars at Loines Observatory.

>TOURIST

9. PROVINCETOWN

Head down to the tip of the Cape for a little American History and see Pilgrim Monument in Provincetown. This monument commemorates the site of the Pilgrims first landing in the New World. Provincetown is also a quaint town. Walk around and enjoy the different shops and restaurants.

10. HYANNIS

Head to Hyannis and visit the John F. Kennedy Hyannis Museum. Here you will experience interactive exhibits, learn about civic engagement and learn about the Kennedy family. The Kennedy compound is in Hyannis. You may be at a cafe for lunch and sitting next to a Kennedy and not even know it.

If you want to learn more about JFK, visit the JFK Library in Boston. When there you can also pop over next door to the Edward M. Kennedy Institute. At the EMKI in Boston you will see a replica of the US Senate Chambers and learn about Senator Ted Kennedy and explore the interesting exhibits about government.

>TOURIST

HISTORICAL SITES

11. LOWELL NATIONAL HISTORICAL PARK

Massachusetts is rich in early American History. While some other parts of the state focus on the Cradle of Liberty, the early days before the American Revolutionary War, Lowell focuses on a different revolution, the Industrial Revolution.

Lowell National Historical Park is located throughout the city. Here you will be able to learn about the textile mills that were built in Lowell and the mill girls and immigrants who toiled many hours to make the textiles.

The Visitor's Center is a great place to begin your tour of the National Historical Park.

You can talk to park rangers, view an informational movie and buy some Lowell merch. It is located at 246 Market Street. Here you can sign up for walking tours or canal tours of the city with a knowledgeable park ranger. Make sure to catch the video presentation while you are at the Visitor's Center.Pick up a map of the city and head out on your historical adventure. While you are there make sure you take advantage of the Trolley inside for a fun photo op!

While it is not part of the National Park, the Brush Art Gallery is located directly across from the Visitor's Center. Stop in and support some local artists.

A trip to Lowell must include the Boott Cotton Mills, also part of the National Historical Park. Here you will learn more about the birth of the Industrial Revolution as you explore the museum. Make sure to cover your ears when you walk through the weave room. Those looms make a lot of noise and only a few of them are running. Imagine the sound that must have been coming from those buildings when all of the looms were turned on. It has been said that the building used to sway from all of the noise of the different machines.

Check out the interactive displays in the museum as well. This is located on the second floor of the mill. Here you will learn about the various jobs in the textile mills, labor reform and may even get a chance to card some cotton. The museum has great displays and interactive exhibits to learn about the working conditions the mill girls faced daily and what they did to improve conditions.

>TOURIST

Now that you have learned how the mill girls labored in the textile mills, walk through the boardinghouse to learn how they lived. You will see an example of what a kitchen and dining room looked like as well as their sleeping quarters. Here you can find out how girls spent

their free time from the hours of 7:00 PM to 10:00 PM.

Up on the second floor of the boarding house is an exhibit of a petition that was created by the girls to improve their working conditions. One wall has a petition and all of the names of the people who signed it.

During the summer at Boarding house park you can find free kid friendly entertainment on Wednesday or Thursday mornings. Bring a blanket and make a picnic out of it. Your little ones will enjoy a variety of children's entertainers. If it rains, the show is moved to the high school auditorium across the street.

Boardinghouse Park also offers a concert series during the summer. This is known as the Lowell Summer Music Series. Tickets range in price starting from approximately $45.00 on up. Lots of famous people have played at Boardinghouse Park. Pat Benetar and The B52s to name a few. There are also great cover bands. A few summers ago, I saw Peter Frampton there. It was a phenomenal show.

Make sure you bring a lawn chair or a blanket to sit on and some snacks as this is an outdoor venue. Alcohol is prohibited. Oh and another thing, people set up their lawn chairs starting around 8:00 am to make sure they have their spot saved. If you want a good spot, drop your blanket and chairs off in the morning and spend the rest of your day exploring the area. This is a great place to see a show. Just like the children's shows if there is inclement weather, the concert is moved across the street to the high school.

Stroll through Lucy Larcom Park and look at the many sculptures dedicated to the hard working Mill Girls and their struggle to reduce the work day from fourteen hours to ten. On Fridays

during the summer months check out the Farmers' Market at Lucy Larcom. Lucy Larcom Park is located between the two main buildings of the high school along the canal. You will know you are in the right spot if you look up and see the bridges that connect the two high school buildings. They always

>TOURIST

reminded me of a hamster tube. You will see why when you look at them.

Lowell is so much more than a National Historic Park. There are lots of art galleries and studios. Lowell has a wide variety of delicious ethnic restaurants to try.

12. LEXINGTON AND CONCORD

Head on over to Minuteman National Historical Park. There you will learn about the first battle of the American Revolution on April 19, 1775. The Park is open from sunrise to sunset. At the Minuteman Visitor's Center located at 250 North Great Road, Lincoln, MA, you will experience a multimedia presentation to learn about hours leading up to and about the first battle of the American Revolution. The Visitor's Center has a little store and a small exhibit to explore as well.

Outside walk around to explore Battle Road. Step into the footsteps of Minutemen and learn more about the battle at Lexington and Concord. Along Battle Road you will see authentic eighteenth century homes such as Hartwell Tavern. Programs at Hartwell Tavern are available from late June to the end of October.

Next drive over to Northbridge and the Northbridge Visitor's Center. The Visitor's Center is located at 174 Liberty Street, Concord, MA. It is open from April to October. A short walk down the hill will take you to the famous bridge where the colonists routed the British soldiers. Talk to the Park Rangers, they are very knowledgeable. You may even see a presentation of a musket being fired.

Concord has more to offer than the American Revolutionary War. The town of Concord was home to many literary greats in the 1800s. The Old Manse is right next to the Old North Bridge. It was the literary center of Concord at one point. At one point it was home to Ralph Waldo Emerson and then Nathaniel Hawthorne. If you get a chance to enter the Old Manse make sure you look carefully at some of the windows. Nathaniel Hawthorne and his wife Sophia etched poetic messages to each other with a diamond. Visit the homes of Luisa May Alcott, Ralph Waldo Emerson, Nathaniel Hawthorne and Henry David Thoureau, learn about Transcendentalism and see how they lived. You can even visit their final resting places at Sleepy Hollow Cemetery over at Author's Ridge. Head over to Walden Pond, made famous by Thoureau's book Walden. Take a refreshing dip in the pond during the summer. A walk around the pond will bring you to the site of Thoureau's cabin and leave a cairn there in honor of the great author. You may even get a chance

>TOURIST

to meet Henry David Thoureau at a replica of his cabin near the parking lot.

13. FREEDOM TRAIL

The Freedom Train in Boston is a 2.5 mile route marked by a red line. This route will take you to sixteen historic sites around Boston. You will see where the Boston Massacre happened on March 5, 1770, visit the home of Paul Revere and see Old North Church among the many historical stops.

You can take a guided tour of the Freedom Trail or download the map and explore Boston on your own. Just follow the red brick in the road.

Make sure you have plenty of time to step off of the Freedom Trail and explore other historic sites like the Black Heritage Trail. The Black Heritage Trail will take you to fourteen locations where you will learn about the early African American experience in Boston.

14. OLD STURBRIDGE VILLAGE

Old Sturbridge Village is located at 1Old Sturbridge Village Road in Sturbridge, MA in the Western part of the state. Current rates are $28 for adults, $26 for seniors 55 and older, $14 for college students with a valid id and for youths ages 4-14. Children three and under are free. Hours of admission vary from season to season.

At Old Sturbridge Village you will visit a rural 1830s New England Village. As you walk through the village you will have an immersive historical experience. Talk to the costumed interpreters, visit the shops, farms and see the artisans working on the different trades.

15. ADAMS NATIONAL HISTORICAL PARK

Adams National Historical Park is located south of Boston at 1250 Hancock Street, Quincy, MA. Here you will learn about the birthplace of President John Adams and his family. At the Visitor's Center you will be able to take a guided tour. Cost of the tour is $15 and children 16 and younger are free. The guided tour will last about three hours.

>TOURIST

16. SALEM

Head over to Salem, MA for a witchy good time. Here you will see where the beloved television comedy, Bewitched, filmed it's seventh season in 1970 (look for the Samantha Stevens statue). Scenes from Bette Midler's movie, Hocus Pocus, were filmed in and around Salem in 1993. Salem is a lot of fun especially in October. The closer to Halloween the crazier Salem is.

You will certainly learn about the Salem Witch Trials when you visit Gallows Hill Museum and Theater, The Salem Witch Museum or Salem Witch Village and any of the other museums dedicated to the Salem Witch Trials, but Salem, MA is more than witches.

Visit Pioneer Village, a living history museum, located at 310 West Avenue, Salem, MA. Here you will experience what the village of Salem was like in 1630.

The House of Seven Gables at 115 Derby Street in Salem is the setting of a novel by Nataniel Hawthorne by the same name.

Also on Derby Street you will find the Salem Maritime National Historic Site. Here you will learn about sailors and traders as they arrived with a variety of riches from the far east.

17. DEERFIELD

Visit historic Deerfield out in Western Massachusetts. Here you will find another quaint eighteenth century village. Deerfield's history is one of great sorrow and heartache. Deerfield was raided many times by local Indian Villages. On February 29, 1704 the village of Deerfield faced a devastating raid that left 50 people dead and 112 taken into captivity and brought to Canada.

Deerfield works very hard to preserve their heritage. Walk down the center of town and explore some of the original houses to learn about the perseverance of the townspeople.

18. PLYMOUTH PLANTATION

When you visit Plymouth, MA you will have the opportunity to see a seventeenth century replica of the village of Plymouth. Here you will see costumed interpreters who have assumed the roles of real residents of the Plymouth colony. Don't be surprised if they seem confused by your 21st century ways as they take their roles very seriously.

Explore the Mayflower II is a full scale replica of the Mayflower, the ship that brought the Pilgrims and strangers to the New World in 1620.

>TOURIST

Visit the Wampanoag Homesite on the Eel River and learn about the Native people that lived here in the 1600s. Unlike the English village, the staff here are all Native People. Don't be afraid to ask questions as you visit the village.

Plymouth Plantation and its surrounding exhibits are seasonal. Make sure to check to see when they are open. Don't forget to take a gander at Plymouth Rock while you are there.

>TOURIST

MUSEUMS

19. MUSEUM OF FINE ARTS

Located in Boston at 465 Huntington Avenue, the MFA is a beloved museum with many different galleries. Here you can visit the ancient world, see early American treasures all in one day. The MFA has a permanent collection as well as visiting exhibits. It is always an exciting place to visit.

When my boys were little, their preschool did a unit on impressionist paintings. My 3 year old could rattle off facts about Henri Matisse until the cows came home. Each class focused on a painter and as part of the unit, the children recreated a famous painting as an art project.

Around this same time, the MFA had a traveling exhibit of impressionist painters. I took my young boys to see this exhibit, since many of the paintings and artists they learned about were featured in the exhibit. I remember giving each boy $5.00 to spend there. I thought they would have bought something from the snack bar or gift shop. When we went to the impressionist painter exhibit I rented the headphones for myself so I could listen and learn about the works of art. My boys used their $5.00 to rent the headphones as well. While my older son managed to figure out how to put the right number in and listen, my three year old randomly punched numbers in. I am sure that what he was listening to was not necessarily the painting we were looking at. When I tried to help him he, in all of his 3 year old assertiveness and independence, would not accept any help. He did however continue to walk to each painting, put a number in and listen to the description.

20. ISABELLA STUART GARDNER MUSEUM

The Isabella Stuart Gardener Museum at 25 Evans Way in Boston is an eclectic collection of art owned by Isabella Stuart Gardener from Ancient Rome, Medieval Europe, the Islamic World and Asia. It is also the site of an infamous art theft from March of 1990. Intrigued?I hope so. I was very intrigued the first time I explored this museum.

Enjoy the courtyard and the contemporary art as well. The museum is $20 for adults, $18 for seniors and $13 for students and is closed on Tuesdays.

>TOURIST

21. CHILDREN'S MUSEUM

The Children's Museum in Boston on Congress Street is a favorite of my boys. It is a hands-on interactive museum. The cost is $18 and children under 1 are free.

One of my older son's favorite exhibits in this museum was the Arthur the Aardvark exhibit. He loved both the Arthur the Aardvark books and the PBS television show. We always had to make sure to go and see Arthur whenever we visited the museum.

There is another Children's Museum in Massachusetts. It is much smaller than the one in Boston and is geared towards younger kids around preschool age. It is located in Acton, MA and was always fun to explore the different rooms and play. It is now called the Discovery Museum. This used to be two separate museums. One was the Children's Museum, the other a Science Museum. As of 2018 the two museums have merged into one building with both indoor and outdoor play activities. It is at the same location. Young children are encouraged to explore and play as they move through the different areas of the building. You can plan to visit the museum for a fraction of the cost as the one in Boston.

22. WORCESTER ART MUSEUM

The Worcester Art Museum is located on 55 Salisbury Street, Worcester, MA. Adults are $18, Seniors 65+ are $14 and children seventeen and younger are free.

Make sure to check out the Higgins Armory Collection, the second largest collection of its kind in the United States. Enjoy lunch in the cafe and explore and enjoy the art work!

23. ECOTARIUM

When I was a child, this museum was known as the Worcester Science Museum. I am not sure if that was it's actual name or what my family called it, but I loved it there. It is located at 222 Harrington Way, Worcester, MA. The mission of the Ecotarium is to inspire a passion for science and nature. My favorite exhibit was always the Polar Bear swimming in his enclosure.

>TOURIST

24. NORMAN ROCKWELL MUSEUM

Check out the Saturday Evening Post among his other works of art at the Norman Rockwell Museum in Stockbridge out in the western part of the state. The museum is closed on Tuesdays and Wednesdays. Tickets for adults are $20, seniors, retired military and AAA members are $18 and college students are $10. Children 18 and younger and active military are free.

25. BERKSHIRE MUSEUM

The Berkshire Museum is located at 39 South Street in Pittsfield, MA. Admission for adults is $13, children ages 4-17 are $6 and 3 and under are free. Visit the museum from 10-5 on Monday, Thursday, Friday and Saturday, 12-5 on Sunday. The museum is closed on Tuesdays and Wednesdays.

There are an estimated 35,000 artifacts in the permanent collection at the Berkshire Museum. Here you will learn about the Ancient World, Natural Science, American Art and much much more.

>TOURIST

SPORTS

26. FENWAY PARK

If you love baseball make sure you visit Fenway Park near Kenmore Square in Boston to catch a Red Sox game. Take a tour of beautiful Fenway and learn about Pesky's Pole, the Green Monster and Ted Williams. Tours are available starting at 9:00 and end 3 hours before a game with the last tour at 5:00 PM on non game days.

27. CELTICS

Basketball fans, make sure you head to the TD Garden in Boston to catch a Celtics game. Located above North Station, you can take the commuter rail right into Boston to catch the game. The Garden is home to The Sports Museum, so make sure you head over early to check it out. Admire the parquet floor that the Celtics play on and learn about its interesting history. Watch out for Lucky the Leprechaun

28. BRUINS

Love hockey? Make sure you catch a Bruins game at the Garden, same place the Celtics play, in Boston. Look for the Bobby Orr statue outside and hit the Pro Shop for your Sports gear.

In addition to basketball, hockey and the Sports Museum, the Garden is also a venue for many concerts.

29. REVOLUTION

The New England soccer team, the Revolution, play at Gillette Stadium in Foxborough. Slyde the Fox is the much loved mascot for the Revs. Slyde is a fan of all sports New England, but has been known to trash talk other mascots outside of New England. Listen to the Far Post Podcast for all things Revolution and lots of off topic talk.

30. PATRIOTS

Gillette Stadium is home to the New England Patriots football team. In August during training camp fans line up to watch the Patriots practice. Our beloved team has won the Super Bowl 6 times. Games are

>TOURIST

lots of fun. It can get cold towards the end of the season. It is important to dress accordingly.

Patriots Place is a shopping plaza located next to the stadium. When there is no game, enjoy the shops and restaurants. On game day arrive early and tailgate with the fans.

31. LOWELL SPINNERS

The Lowell Spinners are a minor league baseball team and play at Lelacheur Park in Lowell. The Spinners are part of the NY Penn League and are family friendly games and super fun. Tickets are inexpensive and if you want you can purchase a ticket for a little more money to have access to the Gator Pit where you will get a BBQ meal before the game.

The Spinners have a kids section with blow up slides and activities in between innings. Try and catch a T-Shirt, chase the Canaligator around the bases or answer trivia. There is always some sort of Spinners giveaways and things to do on the concourse.

32. WOO SOX

The Woo Sox, formerly the Paw Sox from Rhode Island, are a minor league team affiliated with the Boston Red Sox. Their inaugural season starts Spring of 2021. They will be playing at Polar Park in Worcester. I am looking forward to attending games here.

>TOURIST

AMUSEMENT

33. SIX FLAGS

Six Flags New England is located in Agawam, MA out in the Western part of the state. When I was a kid, this amusement park went by the name Riverside Amusement Park. While I have not been there since it was Riverside, both of my children have been there several times since changing to Six Flags. When the boys were in Middle School, the Middle School City wide Band, known as Monday Night Band, and the High School Band would play in a yearly competition near Agawam. After the competition the bands would head to Six Flags for the rest of the day. Funny story, while my oldest son was and still is very musically inclined, my younger son's sole motivation for playing in the middle school band was the yearly trip to Six Flags. He played the trombone. Well, he PRETENDED to play the trombone. On stage in concerts, he just moved the slide back and forth. No sound ever came out of it.

34. APEX

Apex is an indoor amusement area in Marlboro, MA. Head here with your kids for laser tag, bumper cars and a ropes course. Of course you can play a round of mini golf, head to the arcade or go bowling here too. This seems to be a one stop place for indoor entertainment.

>TOURIST

CASINOS
35. MGM

Enjoy the Las Vegas experience right here in Springfield, Massachusetts. MGM is a casino and hotel with restaurants and a comedy club. Located in the western part of the state you will be close to the attractions in the Berkshires.

36. ENCORE

Encore Casino is the newest casino in Massachusetts. This casino also brings the Vegas experience here on the east coast. It is located at 1 Broadway in Everett, MA right near Boston.

37. PLAINRIDGE

Plainridge Park Casino is at 301 Washington Street, Plainville,MA heading south on 495 near Rhode Island. This casino is slots and electronic table games. From April to November you can catch live harness horse racing here.

>TOURIST

HIKES

38. QUINCY QUARRY

Quincy Quarry is a unique hiking experience. Once a granite quarry for over a hundred years and the source of stone for the Bunker Hill Monument, Quincy Quarry is a one of a kind place. The twenty-two acres was purchased by Boston's Metropolitan District Commission (MDC) and was filled in with dirt from the Big Dig in Boston (a major highway renovation project in Boston that rerouted the highway). Once the quarry was filled in it became usable by the public for rock climbing activities. The big attraction is on the rocks. It is the ever changing graffiti and artwork spray painted on the cliffs. Up on top of the rocks you can see the skyline of Boston. The Quincy Quarry has also been used for scenes in a few movies set in Boston.

39. PURGATORY CHASM

Purgatory Chasm, 198 Purgatory Road, Sutton, MA is a state park. Walk along several different trails for a wide variety of granite rock formations known as The Pulpit, The Corn Crib, The Coffin, Fat Man's Misery and Lovers' Leap. Who wouldn't want to explore Purgatory Chasm with names like that for the trails. The Chasm is about a quarter of a mile and has walls of granite as high as 70 feet.

According to geologists,Purgatory Chasm is said to have its origin 14,000 year during the end of the ice age when there was a sudden release of dammed up glacial water. Native American Legend has a different story. According to the legend, an Algonquin woman murdered a white settler. Shortly after she encountered who she thought was another white settler and tried to run away. The settler grabbed her and she prayed to the god Hobomoko to save her. Much to her dismay, the white settler turned out to be Hobomoko in disguise. Hobomoko grabbed his captive and flew to Purgatory Chasm. Colonists say the devilish Hobomoko created the chasm that day by his actions against the Algonquin woman. Historians say that the legend was a way for colonists to convert the natives to Christianity by depicting Hobomoko in a devilish way.

Whether you believe the science, history or legend, this is a fascinating place to hike and picnic with your family.

>TOURIST

40. GREAT BROOK FARM

If you love outdoor adventure, make sure to visit Great Brook State Farm in Carlisle, MA. Here at Great Brook Farm there are many hiking trails to explore in the summer. In the winter, enjoy cross country skiing here. They rent the gear if you don't have your own. Check the snow conditions before you head over there to cross country ski. Great Brook Farm is open daily from sunrise to sunset.

Great Brook Farm has over twenty miles of trails and working dairy farm. This is another great place to picnic in the summer. Make sure you stop and get an ice cream before you head out.

>TOURIST

TIPS, TRICKS AND MISCELLANY

41. PURPLE PLUME

The Purple Plume is a women's boutique located on 35 Church Street Lenox, Massachusetts. If you are out in the Berkshires stop into this shop. You won't be disappointed. The Purple Plume describes itself as a place to buy wearable art and handcrafted jewelry. When you get there, ask for the owner. Tell her that her cousin Kathy sent you!

Throughout the state there are lots of little shops and boutiques like the Purple Plume. Make sure to stop in and support small business owners in the state.

42. HOW CAN I BE GOING SOUTH WHEN I AM HEADED NORTH?

In Massachusetts you can be heading south on one highway when you are driving north on another. I know it sounds confusing and it really is not as bad as it seems. Though, I am not sure I quite understand it. There are parts of highway 128 where it merges with other highways. You will see signs that tell you that you are heading north and south at the same time.

Don't panic, as long as you pay attention to the exits and your gps you will be fine.

43. SPEAKING OF HIGHWAYS

Just an FYI, the Mass Pike is a toll road that runs east to west from Boston to the Berkshires through the central part of the state. Route 2 runs east to west as well but takes a northern route. Route 2 is not a toll road. Through the eastern part of the state and running north to south are 495, 93, 95, 128 and for a more scenic route through some coastal towns, route 1. Running north and south in the western part of the state is route 91.

44. RECOMMENDED RESTAURANTS

Massachusetts has many wonderful restaurants to dine in. I have lots of local favorites in and around Lowell, MA. In order to give the best recommendations for the region or area that you are visiting, I am going to defer to the Phantom Gourmet. The Phantom Gourmet is a local television show that highlights local restaurants. The Phantom is an anonymous food critic who visits these establishments then features the restaurant on the

>TOURIST

show. He or she does not disappoint with recommendations. There is a link below that takes you to the Phantom Gourmet site. There you can search for restaurants near you.

I have another shameless plug. If you are in Worcester, head over to Herbie's on Southbridge Street. Here it is all about the atmosphere. It is definitely a local joint. The food is not pricey and seafood is delicious. This establishment is owned by another one of my paternal cousins.

45. PLACES TO STAY

Check out Concord's Colonial Inn in Concord.

Try The Porches Inn in North Adams.

How about the Harbor View Hotel on Martha's Vineyard in Edgartown?

Seven Hills Inn is located in Lenox, MA.

The Red Lion Inn in Stockbridge looks like a great place.

For places to stay check out VRBO or AirBnB for places to rent if you are not interested in staying at one of the many amazing hotels and inns in Massachusetts.

46. LINGO

If you are in Massachusetts you need to talk like a local. Here are a few key terms to help you out:

Head over to Dunks or Dunkins (short for Dunkin' Donuts) for some ice coffee.

Bang a uey- make a u-turn

The Packie, short for the Package Store, a place where you buy alcohol.

The Rotary- It is called a roundabout by most everyone but Massachusetts natives.

Make sure to Drop your R's at the end of words:

Instead of ever say evah

Instead of car say cah

Instead of summer say summah

Instead of water say watah

And add R's to words that don't have them:

Instead of idea say idear

Instead of agenda say agender

>TOURIST

47. TOWNS AND CITIES

The towns and cities in Massachusetts have interesting names and are not pronounced at all how they look.

Worcester is pronounced Woos-ter or if you are a local, Woos-tah.

Haverhill is pronounced Hay-vrill

Leominster is pronounced Lem-on-ster or as the locals say, Lem-on-stah

Concord is pronounced Con-curd

Billerica is pronounced Bill-ric-a

48. WINTERS

Winters can be tough in New England. Some parts of the state are more prone to lots of accumulated snow. If you are here in the winter it can get very cold, especially with the wind chill. Be prepared to dress accordingly. Layers, lots of layers. If you love the winter, there are some good places to go skiing, ice skating and snowshoeing in Massachusetts.

49. SUMMERS

Summers in Massachusetts can be hot and muggy. Make sure to have plenty of sunscreen and water with you even if you are not at the beach. Massachusetts has lots of thunderstorms in the summer months. While we do get tornadoes, they are not as common as they are in other parts of the country. There are many things to do in the summer months from spending a day at one of the many beaches, to taking a Duck Boat ride in Boston. A Duck Boat is an amphibious vehicle that tours Boston on both land and water.

>TOURIST
50. ARRIVING IN THE STATE

With Flying you have a few options. Logan International Airport is in Boston. It is the major airport in the area. However there are other options. Worcester has a small regional airport that is easy to get in and out of quickly. Manchester, NH also has a small regional airport that is fairly easy to get in and out of.

Take the Train into South Station in Boston. You can take commuter trains from South Station or North Station to different parts of the state.

Of course you can always drive or arrive on the bus.

Whatever way you choose to arrive here, Welcome!

DID YOU KNOW?

Jane Adams corresponded with her husband John Adams when he was away at the Constitutional Convention. She famously told him to "remember the ladies" when he was discussing independence from England. Jane Adams is also only one of two women in US history that has been both first lady and a mother of a president of the United States. Barbara Bush is the other. Her correspondence with John Adams can be viewed digitally at the Massachusetts Historical Society.

Johnny Chapman, famously known as Johnny Appleseed, was born in Leominster, MA. He was a pioneer who introduced apple trees to parts of the midwestern United States. Although much of his story is part of the American mythology, he was in fact a real person.

The first chocolate chip cookie, now famously known as Nestle Toll House Cookie, was invented in Whitman, Massachusetts by a woman named Ruth Wakefield. Her cookie was created by accident. As the story goes, Ruth was experimenting in her kitchen of the inn she and her husband owned. She cut up chunks of her Nestle semi sweet Chocolate Bar and added them to the cookie batter. After removing the

>TOURIST

cookies from the oven, Ruth noticed that the bits of chocolate did not melt, instead it gave the cookie an interesting texture and taste. The rest is culinary history.

Some very famous actors have once called Massachusetts home. Matt Damon and Ben Aflect are obvious to most everyone, but did you know that Bette Davis and Jack Lemon once called Massachusetts home?

>TOURIST

OTHER RESOURCES:

Art Galleries- https://art-collecting.com/galleries_ma.htm

Berkshires- https://berkshires.org/

Chronicle a TV show with great ideas for things to do - https://www.wcvb.com/chronicle#

Edward M. Kennedy Institute- https://www.emkinstitute.org/

Hikes and Trails- https://www.alltrails.com/us/massachusetts

John F. Kennedy Library- https://www.jfklibrary.org/

Massachusetts Historical Society- https://www.masshist.org/

More Breweries- https://massbrewersguild.org/

More interesting facts about Massachusetts- https://www.onlyinyourstate.com/massachusetts/11-interesting-weird-facts-ma/

More Museums- https://www.visit-massachusetts.com/state/museums-and-galleries/

Original Toll House Cookie Recipe- https://newengland.com/today/food/original-toll-house-cookies/

Phantom Gourmet Recommended Restaurants- https://www.phantomgourmet.com/

Places to stay- https://www.visitma.com/where-to-stay/

>TOURIST
TRIVIA (JUST FOR FUN!)

1) What is the Capital of Massachusetts?
2) What is the highest point in Massachusetts?
3) What sport was invented in Springfield, Massachusetts in 1891?
4) What happened in Boston, Massachusetts on March 10, 1876?
5) What is Chargoggagoggmanchauggagoggchaubunagungamaugg?
6) What was celebrated for the first time in Plymouth, Massachusetts in 1621?
7) What cookie was named after a Massachusetts town and not a famous scientist?
8) What is Boston Common?
9) What is Mintonette?
10) What was established in Boston, Massachusetts in 1897?

ANSWERS

1) Boston
2) Mt. Greylock at 3,491 feet above sea level
3) Basketball, by James Naismith
4) The first phone call in history
5) The name of a lake in Webster, Massachusetts. It is also the 5th longest word in the world.
6) The First Thanksgiving
7) Fig Newtons were named after Newton, Massachusetts
8) The oldest public park in the United States, originally used for grazing cattle and military exercises.
9) The original name for volleyball, the game was invented in Holyoke, Massachusetts by William G. Morgan in 1895.
10) The country's first subway system

>TOURIST

PACKING AND PLANNING TIPS

A Week before Leaving

- Arrange for someone to take care of pets and water plants.
- Email and Print important Documents.
- Get Visa and vaccines if needed.
- Check for travel warnings.
- Stop mail and newspaper.
- Notify Credit Card companies where you are going.
- Passports and photo identification is up to date.
- Pay bills.
- Copy important items and download travel Apps.
- Start collecting small bills for tips.
- Have post office hold mail while you are away.
- Check weather for the week.
- Car inspected, oil is changed, and tires have the correct pressure.
- Check airline luggage restrictions.
- Download Apps needed for your trip.

Right Before Leaving

- Contact bank and credit cards to tell them your location.
- Clean out refrigerator.
- Empty garbage cans.
- Lock windows.
- Make sure you have the proper identification with you.
- Bring cash for tips.
- Remember travel documents.
- Lock door behind you.
- Remember wallet.
- Unplug items in house and pack chargers.
- Change your thermostat settings.
- Charge electronics, and prepare camera memory cards.

\>TOURIST

READ OTHER GREATER THAN A TOURIST BOOKS

Greater Than a Tourist- California: 50 Travel Tips from Locals

Greater Than a Tourist- Salem Massachusetts USA 50 Travel Tips from a Local by Danielle Lasher

Greater Than a Tourist United States: 50 Travel Tips from Locals

Greater Than a Tourist- St. Croix US Birgin Islands USA: 50 Travel Tips from a Local by Tracy Birdsall

Greater Than a Tourist- Montana: 50 Travel Tips from a Local by Laurie White

Children's Book: Charlie the Cavalier Travels the World by Lisa Rusczyk Ed. D.

> TOURIST

Follow us on Instagram for beautiful travel images:
http://Instagram.com/GreaterThanATourist

Follow *Greater Than a Tourist* on Amazon.

CZYKPublishing.com

> TOURIST

At *Greater Than a Tourist*, we love to share travel tips with you. How did we do? What guidance do you have for how we can give you better advice for your next trip? Please send your feedback to GreaterThanaTourist@gmail.com as we continue to improve the series. We appreciate your constructive feedback. Thank you.

>TOURIST

METRIC CONVERSIONS

TEMPERATURE

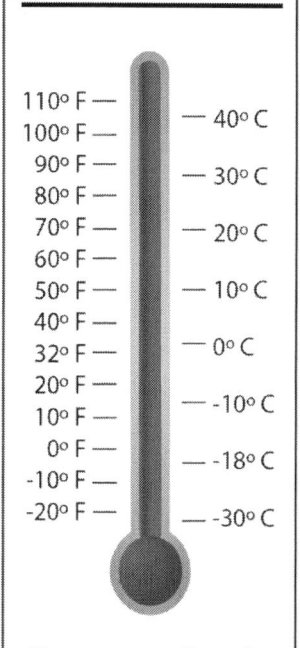

110° F — 40° C
100° F
90° F — 30° C
80° F
70° F — 20° C
60° F
50° F — 10° C
40° F
32° F — 0° C
20° F
10° F — -10° C
0° F
-10° F — -18° C
-20° F — -30° C

To convert F to C:
Subtract 32, and then multiply by 5/9 or .5555.

To Convert C to F:
Multiply by 1.8 and then add 32.

32F = 0C

LIQUID VOLUME

To Convert:.................Multiply by
U.S. Gallons to Liters................. 3.8
U.S. Liters to Gallons 26
Imperial Gallons to U.S. Gallons 1.2
Imperial Gallons to Liters....... 4.55
Liters to Imperial Gallons 22

1 Liter = .26 U.S. Gallon
1 U.S. Gallon = 3.8 Liters

DISTANCE

To convert ....Multiply by
Inches to Centimeters 2.54
Centimeters to Inches 39
Feet to Meters...................... .3
Meters to Feet 3.28
Yards to Meters 91
Meters to Yards 1.09
Miles to Kilometers 1.61
Kilometers to Miles............ .62

1 Mile = 1.6 km
1 km = .62 Miles

WEIGHT

1 Ounce = .28 Grams
1 Pound = .4555 Kilograms
1 Gram = .04 Ounce
1 Kilogram = 2.2 Pounds

>TOURIST
TRAVEL QUESTIONS

- Do you bring presents home to family or friends after a vacation?
- Do you get motion sick?
- Do you have a favorite billboard?
- Do you know what to do if there is a flat tire?
- Do you like a sun roof open?
- Do you like to eat in the car?
- Do you like to wear sun glasses in the car?
- Do you like toppings on your ice cream?
- Do you use public bathrooms?
- Did you bring a cell phone and does it have power?
- Do you have a form of identification with you?
- Have you ever been pulled over by a cop?
- Have you ever given money to a stranger on a road trip?
- Have you ever taken a road trip with animals?
- Have you ever gone on a vacation alone?
- Have you ever run out of gas?

- If you could move to any place in the world, where would it be?
- If you could travel anywhere in the world, where would you travel?
- If you could travel in any vehicle, which one would it be?
- If you had three things to wish for from a magic genie, what would they be?
- If you have a driver's license, how many times did it take you to pass the test?
- What are you the most afraid of on vacation?
- What do you want to get away from the most when you are on vacation?
- What foods smell bad to you?
- What item do you bring on ever trip with you away from home?
- What makes you sleepy?
- What song would you love to hear on the radio when you're cruising on the highway?
- What travel job would you want the least?
- What will you miss most while you are away from home?
- What is something you always wanted to try?

>TOURIST

- What is the best road side attraction that you ever saw?
- What is the farthest distance you ever biked?
- What is the farthest distance you ever walked?
- What is the weirdest thing you needed to buy while on vacation?
- What is your favorite candy?
- What is your favorite color car?
- What is your favorite family vacation?
- What is your favorite food?
- What is your favorite gas station drink or food?
- What is your favorite license plate design?
- What is your favorite restaurant?
- What is your favorite smell?
- What is your favorite song?
- What is your favorite sound that nature makes?
- What is your favorite thing to bring home from a vacation?
- What is your favorite vacation with friends?
- What is your favorite way to relax?
- Where is the farthest place you ever traveled in a car?

- Where is the farthest place you ever went North, South, East and West?
- Where is your favorite place in the world?
- Who is your favorite singer?
- Who taught you how to drive?
- Who will you miss the most while you are away?
- Who if the first person you will contact when you get to your destination?
- Who brought you on your first vacation?
- Who likes to travel the most in your life?
- Would you rather be hot or cold?
- Would you rather drive above, below, or at the speed limited?
- Would you rather drive on a highway or a back road?
- Would you rather go on a train or a boat?
- Would you rather go to the beach or the woods?

>TOURIST

TRAVEL BUCKET LIST

1.

2.

3.

4.

5.

6.

7.

8.

9.

10.

>TOURIST

NOTES

Made in United States
Orlando, FL
21 April 2023